S

Simple

Spanish

Spanish-English
Identical and Similar Words

Des Meagher
Beverley Roberts

Super Simple Spanish ™

This edition first published in 2007.

ISBN 978-0-9552198-1-8

Printed and bound by The Russell Press
Ltd., Nottingham NG6 0BT, UK.

For more information about Super Simple
Spanish please see our website.

www.supersimplespanish.com

Contents

Introduction

Super Simple Spanish is designed to make learning Spanish as simple as possible.

The easiest place to start is identical and similar words in Spanish and English.

Spanish Words
has over 1,000 useful Spanish words. Every single word is identical or very similar in English.

Spanish Sounds
explains the most important sounds in Spanish pronunciation and how word stress is used in Spanish.

Spain
has a map of Spain and the guide we recommend to this beautiful country.

PLEASE NOTE

The **Spanish Words** section has many Spanish words that end in **o**. Words ending in **o** are usually masculine in Spanish.

There are many words that end in **a** in Spanish and these words are usually feminine.

Some Spanish words can end in **o** or **a** if they are used in the masculine and the feminine. For example,

> adult**o** = adult man
> adult**a** = adult woman

> american**o** = American male
> american**a** = American female

To keep the **Spanish Words** section as simple as possible we have used the masculine ending **o** for words that can be used in the masculine and the feminine.

SPANISH WORDS

Identical Spanish-English Words

Similar Spanish-English Words

to accept	aceptar
to adapt	adaptar
to adjust	ajustar
to admire	admirar
to affect	afectar
to approve	aprobar
to authorize	autorizar

accent	acento
acceptable	aceptable
access	acceso
accident	accidente
action	acción
actor	actor
actress	actriz
additional	adicional
adjective	adjetivo
adult	adulto

adventure	aventura
Africa	África
African	africano
agency	agencia
agent	agente
air	aire
air-conditioning	aire acondicionado
airport	aeropuerto
alarm	alarma
alcohol	alcohol

alert	alerta
allergic	alérgico
allergy	alergia
ambulance	ambulancia
American	americano
anchovy	anchoa
animal	animal
anniversary	aniversario
annual	anual
anorak	anorak

antibiotic	antibiótico
antiseptic	antiséptico
appetite	apetito
applicable	aplicable
April	abril
architect	arquitecto
art	arte
arthritis	artritis
artificial	artificial
artist	artista

aspirin	aspirina
asthma	asma
attractive	atractivo
August	agosto
Australia	Australia
Australian	australiano
authentic	auténtico
author	autor
automatic	automático
avenue	avenida

B

to baptize	bautizar
to base	basar
to benefit	beneficiar
to block	bloquear
to bottle	embotellar
to box	boxear
to boycott	boicotear

baby	bebé
bacon	bacon
balcony	balcón
ball	balón
ballet	ballet
bank	banco
bar	bar
barbecue	barbacoa
barrel	barril
barrier	barrera

base	base
bat	bate
beige	beige
bicycle	bicicleta
bike	bici
bikini	biquini
bingo	bingo
block	bloque
blouse	blusa
boot	bota

bottle	botella
boulevard	bulevar
Brazil	Brasil
Brazilian	brasileño
breeze	brisa
British	británico
bronchitis	bronquitis
bus	autobús
butane	butano
button	botón

C

to cancel	cancelar
to confirm	confirmar
to connect	conectar
to consult	consultar
to continue	continuar
to copy	copiar
to cost	costar

cable	cable
caffeine	cafeína
calcium	calcio
calculator	calculadora
calendar	calendario
calm	calma
calorie	caloría
camper	campista
campsite	camping
Canary Islands	Islas Canarias

cancellation	cancelación
candidate	candidato
capacity	capacidad
capital	capital
captain	capitán
carburettor	carburador
carnival	carnaval
carpenter	carpintero
casino	casino
castle	castillo

category	categoría
cathedral	catedral
Catholic	católico
cauliflower	coliflor
caution	cautela
cave	cueva
celebration	celebración
centenary	centenario
centigrade	centígrado
centilitre	centilitro

centimetre	centímetro
central	céntrico
centre	centro
ceremony	ceremonia
champion	campeón
chaos	caos
character	carácter
charity	caridad
cheque	cheque
chimney	chimenea

China	China
Chinese	chino
chlorine	cloro
chocolate	chocolate
cholesterol	colesterol
cigarette	cigarrillo
cinema	cine
circle	círculo
circular	circular
circus	circo

classic	clásico
clementine	clementina
client	cliente
climate	clima
clinic	clínica
club	club
coast	costa
cocktail	cóctel
codeine	codeína
colleague	colega

colour	color
commission	comisión
committee	comité
community	comunidad
compact	compacto
compact disc	disco compacto
concert	concierto
confidential	confidencial
confirmation	confirmación
connection	conexión

consecutive	consecutivo
construction	construcción
consumer	consumidor
contents	contenido
context	contexto
continent	continente
contract	contrato
copy	copia
correct	correcto
cost	coste

coupon	cupón
course	curso
crisis	crisis
cruel	cruel
crucial	crucial
cultural	cultural
culture	cultura
curriculum vitae	currículum vitae
curtain	cortina
cyclist	ciclista

D

to decide	decidir
to depend	depender
to describe	describir
to detect	detectar
to disconnect	desconectar
to disinfect	desinfectar
to divide	dividir

data	datos
database	base de datos
debate	debate
debit	débito
decade	década
decaffeinated	descafeinado
December	diciembre
decision	decisión
decoration	decoración
defect	defecto

deficit	déficit
delicate	delicado
delicious	delicioso
dentist	dentista
deodorant	desodorante
department	departamento
description	descripción
design	diseño
detail	detalle
detector	detector

detergent	detergente
diagram	diagrama
diameter	diámetro
dictionary	diccionario
diet	dieta
different	diferente
difficult	difícil
digital	digital
dimension	dimensión
direct	directo

disc	disco
disconnection	desconexión
discotheque	discoteca
discount	descuento
disinfectant	desinfectante
dispute	disputa
distance	distancia
distributor	distribuidor
divided	dividido
divorce	divorcio

document	documento
dollar	dólar
dose	dosis
double	doble
doughnut	donut
dozen	docena
dune	duna
duplicate	duplicado
duration	duración
dynamo	dinamo

E

to educate	educar
to employ	emplear
to enter	entrar
to escape	escapar
to exist	existir
to explain	explicar
to extend	extender

east	este
economic	económico
edition	edición
education	educación
effect	efecto
effective	eficaz
efficient	eficiente
electrician	electricista
electricity	electricidad
elegant	elegante

employee	empleado
employer	empleador
employment	empleo
energy	energía
enormous	enorme
enthusiasm	entusiasmo
entry	entrada
equipment	equipamiento
equivalent	equivalente
euro	euro

Europe	Europa
European	europeo
European Union	Unión Europea
exact	exacto
excellent	excelente
except	excepto
exception	excepción
excess	exceso
excessive	excesivo
exclusive	exclusivo

excursion	excursión
excuse	excusa
executive	ejecutivo
expatriate	expatriado
experience	experiencia
expert	experto
explanation	explicación
express	expreso
expression	expresión
extreme	extremo

F

to fascinate	fascinar
to finance	financiar
to fix	fijar
to flirt	flirtear
to float	flotar
to fluctuate	fluctuar
to format	formatear

facial	facial
false	falso
false alarm	falsa alarma
fame	fama
family	familia
famous	famoso
fantastic	fantástico
fascinating	fascinante
fatigue	fatiga
favour	favor

fax	fax
February	febrero
ferry	ferry
festival	festival
fibre	fibra
final	final
finalist	finalista
finance	finanzas
fixed	fijo
flexible	flexible

florist's	floristería
fluoride	fluoruro
football	fútbol
footballer	futbolista
format	formato
foundation	fundación
founder	fundador
fraction	fracción
fracture	fractura
fragile	frágil

France	Francia
franchise	franquicia
fraud	fraude
frequent	frecuente
fresh	fresco
frontier	frontera
fruit	fruta
frustrating	frustrante
fundamental	fundamental
future	futuro

G

to gallop	galopar
to generalize	generalizar
to generate	generar
to govern	gobernar
to grease	engrasar
to guarantee	garantizar
to guide	guiar

garage	garaje
garden	jardín
gardener	jardinero
gas	gas
gel	gel
general	general
generator	generador
gin	ginebra
gin and tonic	gin-tonic
ginseng	ginseng

gloss	glosa
glucose	glucosa
gluten	gluten
goal	gol
golf	golf
golfer	golfista
golf club	club de golf
government	gobierno
gradual	gradual
gram	gramo

grammar	gramática
granite	granito
Great Britain	Gran Bretaña
Greece	Grecia
group	grupo
guarantee	garantía
guide	guía
guitar	guitarra
gymnasium	gimnasio
gymnast	gimnasta

H

to hallucinate	alucinar
to harmonize	armonizar
to hibernate	hibernar
to honour	honrar
to hospitalize	hospitalizar
to humiliate	humillar
to hypnotize	hipnotizar

hamburger	hamburguesa
helicopter	helicóptero
hernia	hernia
hero	héroe
heroic	heroico
historic	histórico
history	historia
hobby	hobby
honesty	honestidad
honour	honor

horizon	horizonte
horror	horror
hospital	hospital
hospitality	hospitalidad
hostile	hostil
hotel	hotel
human	humano
hygienic	higiénico
hyperactive	hiperactivo
hypertension	hipertensión

I

to imagine	imaginar
to include	incluir
to inform	informar
to insist	insistir
to inspect	inspeccionar
to install	instalar
to invite	invitar

ideal	ideal
identical	idéntico
identification	identificación
identity	identidad
illegal	ilegal
immediate	inmediato
immigrant	inmigrante
impact	impacto
important	importante
impossible	imposible

impressive	impresionante
incentive	incentivo
incident	incidente
including	incluido
incorrect	incorrecto
incredible	increíble
independent	independiente
indigestion	indigestión
individual	individual
industry	industria

inevitable	inevitable
infection	infección
inflammable	inflamable
inflammation	inflamación
inflation	inflación
influence	influencia
informal	informal
information	información
ingredient	ingrediente
inhaler	inhalador

initial	inicial
initiative	iniciativa
injection	inyección
innocent	inocente
innovation	innovación
insect	insecto
inspection	inspección
inspector	inspector
instinct	instinto
institute	instituto

insulin	insulina
insult	insulto
intelligent	inteligente
intense	intenso
interest	interés
interesting	interesante
internal	interno
international	internacional
Internet	Internet
interpreter	intérprete

inventory	inventario
investigation	investigación
investor	inversor
invisible	invisible
invitation	invitación
irregular	irregular
island	isla
Italian	italiano
Italy	Italia
itinerary	itinerario

J

to justify	justificar
Japan	Japón
Japanese	japonés
jazz	jazz
judo	judo
July	julio
June	junio

K

ketchup	catchup
kilo	kilo
kilobyte	kilobyte
kilogram	kilogramo
kilometre	kilómetro
kilowatt	kilovatio
kiwi fruit	kiwi

L

to laminate	laminar
to legalize	legalizar
to legislate	legislar
to liberate	liberar
to limit	limitar
to locate	localizar
to lubricate	lubricar

laboratory	laboratorio
lamp	lámpara
laser	láser
leader	líder
legal	legal
legislation	legislación
lemon	limón
ligament	ligamento
lime	lima
limit	límite

linen	lino
liqueur	licor
liquid	líquido
list	lista
literature	literatura
litre	litro
logo	logotipo
lotion	loción
lottery	lotería
lubricant	lubricante

M

to march	marchar
to memorize	memorizar
to mention	mencionar
to minimize	minimizar
to modernize	modernizar
to modify	modificar
to multiply	multiplicar

macaroni	macarrones
machine	máquina
mandarin	mandarina
mango	mango
manners	maneras
map	mapa
March	marzo
margarine	margarina
marzipan	mazapán
massage	masaje

mast	mástil
mathematics	matemáticas
maximum	máximo
May	mayo
mayonnaise	mayonesa
mechanic	mecánico
Mediterranean	mediterráneo
melon	melón
member	miembro
memory	memoria

menthol	mentol
messenger	mensajero
method	método
metre	metro
microchip	microchip
microphone	micrófono
milligram	miligramo
millimetre	milímetro
million	millón
minimum	mínimo

minute	minuto
mixed	mixto
model	modelo
modem	módem
modern	moderno
moment	momento
monument	monumento
mosquito	mosquito
motorcycle	motocicleta
mountain	montaña

mountain bike	bicicleta de montaña
much	mucho
multimedia	multimedia
municipal	municipal
muscle	músculo
muscular	muscular
museum	museo
music	música
musician	músico
mustard	mostaza

N

to narrate	narrar
to naturalize	naturalizar
to negotiate	negociar
to normalize	normalizar
to notice	notar
to notify	notificar
to number	numerar

nation	nación
national	nacional
natural	natural
nature	naturaleza
necessary	necesario
negative	negativo
negotiable	negociable
negotiation	negociación
nerve	nervio
nervous	nervioso

nicotine	nicotina
normal	normal
north	norte
north-east	noreste
note	nota
novel	novela
novelist	novelista
November	noviembre
number	número
nylon	nailon

O

to observe	observar
to obstruct	obstruir
to obtain	obtener
to offend	ofender
to offer	ofrecer
to omit	omitir
to organize	organizar

object	objeto
obligation	obligación
obstacle	obstáculo
obstruction	obstrucción
obvious	obvio
ocean	océano
October	octubre
office	oficina
official	oficial
opinion	opinión

optician's	óptica
optimist	optimista
option	opción
orchestra	orquesta
order	orden
organization	organización
organized	organizado
origin	origen
original	original
oxygen	oxígeno

P

to pass	pasar
to photograph	fotografiar
to practise	practicar
to prefer	preferir
to prepare	preparar
to promise	prometer
to publish	publicar

packet	paquete
page	página
painter	pintor
pair	par
palace	palacio
pale	pálido
palm	palma
paper	papel
paracetamol	paracetamol
parallel	paralelo

park	parque
part	parte
partial	parcial
passion	pasión
passport	pasaporte
patience	paciencia
patient	paciente
pause	pausa
pear	pera
pearl	perla

penicillin	penicilina
peninsula	península
per cent	por ciento
perfect	perfecto
perfection	perfección
perfume	perfume
period	periodo
permanent	permanente
permission	permiso
person	persona

personal	personal
pessimist	pesimista
pharmacy	farmacia
phase	fase
photocopier	fotocopiadora
photocopy	fotocopia
photograph	fotografía
photographer	fotógrafo
physical	físico
piano	piano

picnic	picnic
piece	pieza
pilot	piloto
pine	pino
pineapple	piña
plan	plan
plastic	plástico
plate	plato
poem	poema
poet	poeta

point	punto
police	policía
pollen	polen
polyester	poliéster
popular	popular
portion	porción
positive	positivo
possibility	posibilidad
possible	posible
postcode	código postal

potato	patata
power	poder
practice	práctica
preferable	preferible
present	presente
president	presidente
pressure	presión
prince	príncipe
princess	princesa
priority	prioridad

private	privado
probability	probabilidad
probable	probable
problem	problema
process	proceso
product	producto
programme	programa
progress	progreso
project	proyecto
projector	proyector

promise	promesa
pronunciation	pronunciación
protein	proteína
province	provincia
provisional	provisional
publicity	publicidad
pulse	pulso
punctual	puntual
pure	puro
pyjamas	pijama

Q

qualified	cualificado
quality	calidad
quantity	cantidad
quarantine	cuarentena
quarter	cuarto
quarter-finals	cuartos de final
questionnaire	cuestionario

R

to receive	recibir
to recharge	recargar
to reduce	reducir
to repeat	repetir
to represent	representar
to rescue	rescatar
to reserve	reservar

radiator	radiador
radical	radical
radio	radio
ramp	rampa
ray	rayo
reasonable	razonable
receipt	recibo
recent	reciente
recently	recientemente
reception	recepción

receptionist	recepcionista
reflex	reflejo
reform	reforma
refreshing	refrescante
region	región
regional	regional
registration	registro
regular	regular
religion	religión
remote	remoto

rescue	rescate
reservation	reserva
resident	residente
responsible	responsable
restaurant	restaurante
result	resultado
rhythm	ritmo
rich	rico
ridiculous	ridículo
rival	rival

rock	roca
roll	rollo
rose	rosa
route	ruta
routine	rutina
rumour	rumor
rural	rural
Russia	Rusia
Russian	ruso
rustic	rústico

S

to separate	separar
to serve	servir
to simplify	simplificar
to ski	esquiar
to sterilize	esterilizar
to study	estudiar
to supervise	supervisar

saccharin	sacarina
salary	salario
salmon	salmón
salt	sal
sandal	sandalia
sardine	sardina
satellite	satélite
satin	satén
satisfied	satisfecho
sauna	sauna

science	ciencia
second	segundo
section	sección
semi-final	semifinal
sensational	sensacional
sensor	sensor
separate	separado
September	septiembre
series	serie
serious	serio

service	servicio
serviette	servilleta
shampoo	champú
sign	signo
silence	silencio
simple	simple
situation	situación
snob	esnob
sociable	sociable
social security	seguridad social

sofa	sofá
software	software
soldier	soldado
solid	sólido
sorbet	sorbete
soup	sopa
soya	soja
space	espacio
spaghetti	espagueti
special	especial

specialist	especialista
specific	específico
spectator	espectador
spice	especia
spinach	espinaca
splendid	espléndido
sponge	esponja
stable	estable
stadium	estadio
station	estación

statue	estatua
stereo	estéreo
stereotype	estereotipo
sterile	estéril
steroid	esteroide
stomach	estómago
stress	estrés
student	estudiante
studio	estudio
style	estilo

subscriber	suscriptor
subtitle	subtítulo
subtle	sutil
successive	sucesivo
sufficient	suficiente
superficial	superficial
supermarket	supermercado
superstition	superstición
supervision	supervisión
supervisor	supervisor

supplement	suplemento
surfer	surfista
surprise	sorpresa
sustainable	sostenible
syllable	sílaba
symptom	síntoma
syndrome	síndrome
synthetic	sintético
system	sistema
systematic	sistemático

T

to tattoo	tatuar
to televise	televisar
to toast	tostar
to transform	transformar
to traumatize	traumatizar
to trivialize	trivializar
to trot	trotar

talc	talco
talent	talento
taxi	taxi
technician	técnico
technique	técnica
technology	tecnología
telephone	teléfono
teletext	teletexto
television	televisión
temperature	temperatura

temptation	tentación
tendon	tendón
tennis	tenis
tense	tenso
tension	tensión
terminal	terminal
terrible	terrible
text	texto
textile	textil
theatre	teatro

therapy	terapia
thermostat	termostato
title	título
toast	tostada
toaster	tostador
tobacco	tabaco
tolerant	tolerante
total	total
tourism	turismo
tourist	turista

tournament	torneo
toxic	tóxico
tradition	tradición
traditional	tradicional
traffic	tráfico
tragedy	tragedia
train	tren
transfer	transferencia
transport	transporte
treatment	tratamiento

triumph	triunfo
trivial	trivial
trophy	trofeo
tropical	tropical
trumpet	trompeta
tube	tubo
tubular	tubular
tulip	tulipán
tunnel	túnel
typical	típico

U

to undulate	ondular
to unify	unificar
to unite	unir
to urinate	orinar
to use	usar
to utilize	utilizar

ultimatum	ultimátum
ultrasound	ultrasonido
ultraviolet	ultravioleta
unacceptable	inaceptable
unanimous	unánime
uniform	uniforme
unilateral	unilateral
unit	unidad
universal	universal
university	universidad

university student	universitario
unjust	injusto
unlimited	ilimitado
unnecessary	innecesario
unpopular	impopular
unsatisfactory	insatisfactorio
urban	urbano
urgent	urgente
use	uso
user	usuario

V

to validate	validar
to value	valorar
to varnish	barnizar
to vary	variar
to vibrate	vibrar
to visit	visitar
to vote	votar

valid	válido
valley	valle
value	valor
valve	válvula
vanilla	vainilla
variable	variable
varied	variado
variety	variedad
varnish	barniz
vast	vasto

vegetarian	vegetariano
vehicle	vehículo
vein	vena
ventilation	ventilación
verb	verbo
verbal	verbal
verdict	veredicto
versatile	versátil
version	versión
vertical	vertical

vertigo	vértigo
vet	veterinario
viable	viable
victory	victoria
video	video
vinegar	vinagre
violin	violín
virus	virus
visa	visado
visible	visible

visit	visita
visitor	visitante
vitamin	vitamina
vocabulary	vocabulario
volt	voltio
voltage	voltaje
volume	volumen
volunteer	voluntario
vote	voto
voter	votante

WXYZ

watt	vatio
west	oeste
X-rays	rayos X
yacht	yate
yoghurt	yogur
zero	cero
zoo	zoo

SPANISH SOUNDS

Important
Spanish Sounds

Spanish
Word Stress

Important Spanish Sounds

- ce

In Spanish **ce** is pronounced like the **th** in **th**anks.

Practise saying this **th** sound with these Spanish words.

centígrado	(centigrade)
centímetro	(centimetre)
céntrico	(central)
centro	(centre)
cero	(zero)

Important Spanish Sounds

▪ ci

In Spanish **ci** is pronounced like the **th** in thanks.

Practise saying this **th** sound with these Spanish words.

cigarrillo	(cigarette)
cine	(cinema)
circo	(circus)
circular	(circular)
círculo	(circle)

Important Spanish Sounds

- e

In Spanish e at the end of a word is pronounced like a – the first letter of the English alphabet.

Practise saying this a sound with these Spanish words.

cable	(cable)
enorme	(enormous)
norte	(north)
parte	(part)
simple	(simple)

Important Spanish Sounds

▪ ge

In Spanish **ge** is pronounced like the **ch** in the Scottish word lo**ch**. This is a back-of-the-throat sound as if clearing the throat!

Practise saying this throaty lo**ch** sound with these Spanish words.

gel   (gel)
generador (generator)
general   (general)
generalizar (to generalize)
generar   (to generate)

Important Spanish Sounds

▪ gi

In Spanish **gi** is pronounced like the **ch** in the Scottish word lo**ch**. This is a back-of-the-throat sound as if clearing the throat!

Practise saying this throaty lo**ch** sound with these Spanish words.

Gibraltar   (Gibraltar!)
gigante   (giant)
gimnasio   (gym)
gimnasta   (gymnast)
ginebra   (gin)

Important Spanish Sounds

▪ h

In Spanish **h** has no sound. It is a silent letter.

Practise saying these Spanish words making sure **h** has no sound.

hamburguesa (hamburger)
historia   (history)
honor   (honour)
hospital   (hospital)
hotel   (hotel)

Important Spanish Sounds

▪ j

In Spanish j is pronounced like the ch in the Scottish word loch. This is a back-of-the-throat sound as if clearing the throat!

Practise saying this throaty loch sound with these Spanish words.

Japón	(Japan)
japonés	(Japanese)
jardín	(garden)
julio	(July)
junio	(June)

Important Spanish Sounds

▪ ll

In Spanish **ll** is pronounced like the **y** in **yes**.

Practise saying this **y** sound with these Spanish words.

botella	(bottle)
castillo	(castle)
millón	(million)
rollo	(roll)
valle	(valley)

Important Spanish Sounds

- ñ

In Spanish ñ is pronounced like **ny** in can**y**on.

Practise saying this **ny** sound with these Spanish words.

diseño   (design)
Gran Bretaña(Great Britain)
montaña   (mountain)
piña   (pineapple)

and a very important word
     España   (Spain)

Important Spanish Sounds

■ V

In Spanish v is pronounced like b in big.

Practise saying this b sound with these Spanish words.

valor	(value)
versión	(version)
vertical	(vertical)
vértigo	(vertigo)
vitamina	(vitamin)

Important Spanish Sounds

■ z

In Spanish z is pronounced like the th in thanks.

Practise saying this th sound with these Spanish words.

actriz	(actress)
barniz	(varnish)
marzo	(March)
mostaza	(mustard)
pieza	(piece)

Important Spanish Sounds Summary

ce, ci and z is th in thanks

e at the end of a word is a – the sound of the first letter of the English alphabet.

ge, gi and j is ch in loch

h is silent

ll is y in yes

ñ is ny in canyon

v is b in big

Spanish Word Stress

Spanish words are normally stressed on the last syllable.

actor normal papel popular

But if a Spanish word ends in a, e, i, o, u, s or n, the stress is on the last-but-one syllable.

nota arte plato intenso

If a Spanish word has an accent (') the stress is on the accent

bebé melón teléfono expresión

SPAIN

Recommended Guide
to Spain

Simple Map
of Spain

Recommended Guide to Spain

In over 20 years visiting Spain we've found that the best guide to Spain is the **Michelin (Red) Guide to Hotels and Restaurants**.

The Michelin (Red) Guide manages to find the very best of Spain in every price range and includes:

- Excellent accommodation
- Fantastic tapas bars
- Great restaurants
- Superb maps
- Good tourist information

Updated every year **The Michelin (Red) Guide** covers every corner of Spain and all the islands. In our opinion it is the best guide to **Spain.**

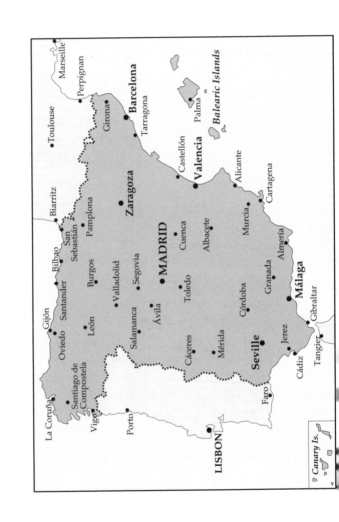